Speaker's Corner Books

is a provocative new series designed to stimulate, educate, and foster discussion on significant public policy topics. Written by experts in a variety of fields, these brief and engaging books should be read by anyone interested in the trends and issues that shape our society.

More thought-provoking titles
in the Speaker's Corner series

Think for Yourself!
An Essay on Cutting through the Babble, the Bias, and the Hype
Steve Hindes

God and Caesar in America
An Essay on Religion and Politics
Gary Hart

The Enduring Wilderness:
Protecting Our Natural Heritage through the Wilderness Act
Doug Scott

Parting Shots from My Brittle Bow:
Reflections on American Politics and Life
Eugene J. McCarthy

The Brave New World of Health Care
Richard D. Lamm

Social Security and the Golden Age:
An Essay on the New American Demographic
George McGovern

For more information, visit our Web site,
www.fulcrumbooks.com

Two Wands, One Nation

an Essay on Race and Community in America

Two Wands, One Nation
an Essay on Race and Community in America

Richard D. Lamm
Former Governor, State of Colorado

 Fulcrum Publishing

Golden, Colorado

Library of Congress Cataloging-in-Publication Data
Two wands, one nation: an essay on race and community in America / by Richard D. Lamm.
     p. cm.
  ISBN 1-55591-585-X (pbk.) 1. African Americans--
Intellectual life. 2. Hispanic Americans--Intellectual life.
3. Minorities--Unites State--Social conditions. 4. Community
life--United States. 5. United States--Race relations.
6. United States--Ethnic relations. I. Title.
  E184.A1 L253 2006
  305.800973--dc22

                                   2005030196

Printed in Canada
0 9 8 7 6 5 4 3 2

Editorial: Sam Scinta
Cover and interior design: Jack Lenzo

Fulcrum Publishing
16100 Table Mountain Parkway, Suite 300
Golden, Colorado 80403
(800) 992-2908 • (303) 277-1623
www.fulcrumbooks.com

To the University of Denver:
May you come to understand that on a
college campus, "too controversial" is not
the answer to anything, ever.

Contents

Introduction 1
Chapter One
  Great Nations Need Great Citizens 14
Chapter Two
  The New Wealth of Nations 24
Chapter Three
  Two Paths 38
Chapter Four
  Are Mexicans Italians? Are Blacks Africans? 45
Chapter Five
  Honor Diversity, but Celebrate Unity 52
Chapter Six
  What Does It Mean to Our Future? 70
Appendix A
  **Typology of Progress-Prone
  and Progress-Resistant Cultures** 76
Appendix B:
  Books That Speak Volumes 78

Introduction

John Gardner once said that higher education was "caught ... between unloving critics and uncritical lovers." To my mind, that clever aphorism applies to discussions about minority status and performance in America. On one hand, there are "unloving critics" who, for a variety of reasons, despair of blacks and Hispanics ever fully joining the American community and pulling their own weight. On the other hand, there are the "uncritical lovers" of minority culture who explain all low performance and minority social problems as the effects of "racism and discrimination." They generally brand all critical comments on minority underperformance as "racism" or "blaming the victim." But America's future, in many important ways, depends on solving the problem of minority underperformance. The growing percentage of blacks and Hispanics who make up our population demands that this discussion not be put off. America is not producing the skills, talents, and educational achievement in its young people to keep us competitive in the new global world. We are fast growing a second underclass, a Hispanic underclass, not having fully solved the problems of the first underclass, blacks. We are overdue for an honest and candid dialogue on race and ethnicity, and all America, including white America, must candidly participate in this dialogue. America deserves no less.

A candid dialogue on minority status has been a long time coming, delayed for some very good reasons. It took a lot of psychic energy and dedication to overcome the deep strain of racism that clearly was in the American society of my youth. This revolution of laws, attitudes, and hearts was nothing less than a social revolution, and revolutions are not known for their nuances or subtleties.

But revolutionary fever is hard to sustain, and it often becomes counterproductive. No society can govern itself in a constant state of revolutionary fever. Balance and objectivity are required to sustain governance. America cannot wait and allow every minority group to self-diagnosis its own problems and come up with its own solutions in isolation from the rest of America. We must make room for some "loving critics" of minority underperformance from outside those communities. All America has a stake in the success of minority America.

This dialogue is not for the faint of heart. This book arose out of an act of censorship by a vice provost at the University of Denver (D.U.), which, while outrageous in itself, was compounded by the failures of either the D.U. provost or the chancellor to overturn that censorship. This book had its genesis in the words "too controversial." Let me explain.

I read one evening a hysterical column in one of D.U.'s in-house publications, *The Source*, finding white

America guilty of "prejudice, racism, and systemic racial oppression" and implying that this was the cause of minority failure patterns. The offending article transported me back to my monthly meetings as governor with the Hispanic caucus in which the only subjects on the table were Hispanic appointments, bilingual education, and affirmative action. There was never even a hint in these meetings that the plight of Hispanics was partly self-imposed. So, to enlarge the menu after having had a solid diet of "victimization," I wrote the following:

Two Wands

Let me offer you, metaphorically, two magic wands that have sweeping powers to change society. With one wand you could wipe out all racism and discrimination from the hearts and minds of white America. The other wand you could wave across the ghettoes and barrios of America and infuse the inhabitants with Japanese or Jewish values, respect for learning, and ambition. But, alas, you can't wave both wands. Only one.

Which would you choose? I understand that many of us would love to wave both wands; no one can easily refuse the chance to erase racism and discrimination. But I suggest that the best wand for society and for those who live in the ghettoes and barrios would be the second wand.

This metaphor is important in correctly diagnosing one of the most significant problems facing contemporary America: the large economic, educational, and employment gap between black/Hispanic America and white/Asian America. The problems of crime, educational failure, drugs, gangs, teenage pregnancy, and unemployment that burden certain groups threaten our collective future. They form a nation-threatening social pathology that must be addressed in broader terms than we have done to date.

Most discussion of minority failure blames racism and discrimination. I'm an old civil rights lawyer, and such racism and discrimination clearly still exists. But the problem, I fear, is deeper than the current dialogue. We need to honestly think about these problems with a new sophistication. One of these new areas is to recognize that, increasingly, scholars are saying that "culture matters."

I'm impressed, for instance, that minorities that have been discriminated against earn the highest family incomes in America. Japanese Americans, Jews, Chinese Americans, and Korean Americans all outearn white America by substantial margins, and all have faced discrimination and racism. We put Japanese Americans in camps sixty years ago and confiscated much of their property. Yet today they outearn all other demographic groups. Discrimination and racism are social cancers and can never be justified, but it is enlightening that, for these groups, they were a hurdle, not a barrier to success.

The Italians, the Irish, the people from the Balkans—America has viewed all these groups and many more with hostility and suspicion, yet all have integrated and succeeded. Hispanic organizations excuse their failure rates solely in terms of discrimination by white America and object vociferously when former education secretary Lauro Cavazos observes that Hispanic parents "don't take enough interest in education." But Cuban Americans have come to America and succeeded brilliantly. Do we discriminate against Hispanics from Mexico but not Hispanics from Cuba?

I suggest that those groups whose culture and values stress delayed gratification—education, hard work, success, and ambition—are those groups that succeed in America, regardless of discrimination. I further suggest that, even if discrimination were removed, other groups would still have massive problems until they developed the traits that lead to success. Asian and Jewish children do twice as much homework as black and Hispanic students and get twice as good grades. Why should we be surprised?

A problem well defined is a problem half solved. We must recognize that all the civil rights laws in the world are not going to solve the problem of minority failure. Ultimately, blacks and Hispanics are going to have to see that their solution is largely in their own hands. Lionel Sosa, one of America's leading Hispanic businessmen, in his book *The Americano Dream*, titles his first chapter "Escaping the Cultural Shackles."

Daniel Patrick Moynihan has insightfully observed, "The central conservative truth is that it is culture, not politics, that determines the success of a society. The central liberal truth is that politics can change a culture and save it from itself."

Thus, morally, I would want badly to wave both wands; if I had to choose, I would wave the second wand. A Confucian or Jewish love of learning would gain minorities far more than any affirmative action laws we might pass.

Jesus Treviño denied permission to reprint the article that I was reacting to. This is a great loss to the reader of this book, because the article is its own best evidence. Treviño believes we must move beyond prejudice and individual racism and look at "the systematic exploitation or oppression of people of color by whites, either knowingly or unknowingly." He claims that whites *as a group* "perpetuate racism in conscious and unconscious ways" and that examples of white racism at work can be found in high poverty rates among American Indians, the lack of minority professors at a university level, large percentages of minorities in janitorial and landscaping positions, and the high school drop-out rates of minorities. He urges more emphasis be placed on "systematic racial oppression" of minorities by whites: "This definition moves away from individual behavior and focuses on large-scale patterns of group discrimination."

Our vice provost for communications turned down this column as "too controversial." "Too controversial," what sad words to hear on an American college campus. The column I tried to respond to is a broadside against all of white America, and I was outraged that this was acceptable to *The Source*, but my answering

> We need a candid public debate about what social glue is necessary to keep diverse people living together in peace. Tragically, one has to risk being called a racist to even begin a discussion.

column was "too controversial." Yet I was not particularly surprised. This response is, sadly, symbolic of attitudes on college campuses across America.

This episode redirected my attention at how hard it is to honestly and candidly discusses problems of minority underperformance—anywhere in America. White America has essentially been excluded from the dialogue. The fear of being called a racist is preventing us from discussing some of the more profound problems in American society. Such fear is paralyzing our national dialogue on myriad immensely important subjects.

I seek an honest dialogue by people of good faith and caring about minority underperformance, diversity, and immigration. We need a candid public debate about what social glue is necessary to keep diverse people living together in peace. Tragically, one has to risk being called a racist to even begin a discussion. This is more than a personal risk; it is a serious threat to

America's future. When we inappropriately use a word like "racist" indiscriminately, we diminish the original meaning of the word. There is a Gresham's law to language, and we do not want to dilute the word because, clearly, there are still racists out there, and it still has valid application.

America is in trouble when it cannot candidly discuss its problems. All great nations have problems, but those problems feed upon themselves when whey cannot be discussed openly and candidly. I believe America will face a time of testing in our immediate future. We shall need to call upon the talents and best efforts of all Americans. We need to honestly address some important issues we have too long avoided. Three deficits—the federal deficit, the trade deficit, and the savings deficit—have locked in a series of economic traumas in the years ahead. Global warming will challenge our political and social structure.

America's new "diversity" raises questions of community, unity, and assimilation. Immigration, which is running four times greater than historical numbers, threatens our environment and is building into America a second underclass when we are already challenged to fully incorporate our existing underclass. The unprecedented disproportion of Spanish-speaking immigrants challenges America's tradition of assimilation, and the historic American melting pot threatens to become a pressure cooker. We will need unity, goodwill, patience, and sacrifice to solve these problems, and these seem in short supply in contemporary America.

Issues of minority underperformance demand

honest debate and reflection, yet there exists on American college campuses a stifling conformity when it comes to race, immigration, and ethnicity. To a large degree, the only acceptable explanation for minority underperformance is racism and discrimination. To observe that part of the fault and part of the correction agenda lie within the minority community itself is immediately challenged as racist and blaming the victim. If some diversity is good, a whole lot more is certainly better, goes the argument, and if you don't agree, you surely must be unenlightened at best, or a closet racist. The liberal agenda demands total loyalty.

> [I]t is becoming increasingly apparent that this problem of minority underperformance is much broader and more nuanced than the impact of racism.

But it is becoming increasingly apparent that this problem of minority underperformance is much broader and more nuanced than the impact of racism. When two-thirds of black births are out-of-wedlock births, it is hard to write a happy or prosperous future for black America. When close to 50 percent of Hispanic students don't graduate from high school, it is hard to see Hispanics following the normal American route to prosperity. Blacks and Hispanics are not succeeding in numbers great enough to keep America competitive, and too often the entire blame is laid at the feet of white America.

Yet when black and Hispanic students do *half* as much homework as Asian and Jewish students and get *half* as good grades, the minority community is itself going to have to take a share of the responsibility. I am increasingly convinced that the key to prosperity for black America and Hispanic America lies mostly in their own hands and through their own efforts. The search for racial justice must be broadened to look inward.

> I am increasingly convinced that the key to prosperity for black America and Hispanic America lies mostly in their own hands and through their own efforts.

It is interesting to me that a similar dialogue is going on in other parts of the world that can help us here. Latin America is rejecting the "dependency" theory that for 100 years blamed most of the problems south of our border on the United States. Traveling in South America in the 1960s, how often we heard, essentially, "Our poverty is your fault!" Slowly, that attitude is changing, and South America is recognizing that most of its problems are self-imposed. An example of this new international candidness is found in a recent Latin American best seller, *Guide to the Perfect Latin American Idiot.* Its authors observe, "In reality—except for cultural factors—nothing prevented Mexico from doing what Japan did when it almost totally displaced the United States' production of television sets."

Increasingly, African intellectuals are recognizing that colonialism is an inadequate explanation for Africa's low level of development. A new honesty and willingness exists among Africans to admit that much of their underdevelopment originated with their own culture and leaders and that the cures are in their own hands. Internationally we see that some cultures are better than others at developing institutions that promote freedom, prosperity, and justice. South America and Africa are asking anew, "What is the path to progress?" More and more nations are turning inward, taking responsibility for their own problems and examining themselves and their own institutions. Less and less are they blaming others. It is a very hopeful trend that I expand upon in chapter two, "The New Wealth of Nations."

Yet in our own country, white America is often intimidated from voicing an opinion on the subject of minority underperformance. At some point in our recent past, this reluctance made white Americans codependents to minority failure. There is a "soft racism of lowered expectations," where majority Americans too often have come to excuse and even to expect lower performance from minority America. We felt guilty in the past—*and we should have felt guilty*, considering our poor racial history.

But public policy is a continuum, and one generation's solutions become another generation's problems. We cannot forever look exclusively to racism. The "minority as victims" was indispensably relevant in the 1950 to 1990 time frame. We needed a great crusade to overcome the legacy of slavery and a culture corrupted by racism. It is still a fight not completely won. But the "victim" model puts all the burden and emphasis on the majority community. It often eclipses the need for minorities themselves to develop habits and disciplines to take advantage of the new, less discriminatory climate. Victimhood has become, in my mind, more of an excuse than an explanation. It was a valid excuse in my youth because no matter their talents, minorities were often precluded from participating in American society. Think Marian Anderson. Think W. E. B. DuBois and Jack Johnson. Think hundreds of millions of lives stunted of their promise. This is America's most historic tragedy and our greatest collective sin. But the vestiges of racism left in our society are now more of a hurdle than barrier. Today the total emphasis on "minorities as victims" is enervating and self-defeating to minorities themselves. It allows minorities to excuse low performance, even when discrimination is not the cause. I believe that the mistaken notion that this is still a pervasively racist society has ironically become one of the chief barriers to the upward mobility of minorities. The "solution," fighting racism, has become the new problem, i.e., the idea the minorities can't get ahead because of our "racist society."

While it is not yet the majority opinion among minority leaders, some brave souls are also speaking out. Black scholar Shelby Steele maintains that blacks' constant focus on being victims keeps minorities

> mired in a victim-focused identity, gives them a disinvestment in success and an investment in failure ... the most pernicious feature of real oppression is that it is always, in itself, an argument that others should be responsible. ... He comes to feel that his individual life will

be improved more by changes in society than by his own initiative. Without realizing it, he makes society rather than himself the agent of change.

We need to rebalance our thinking and reconceptualize the problems and solutions of minority failure. The concept that "I can't succeed because I live in a racist society" has become as serious a problem to twenty-first-century America as racism itself.

Others strongly disagree and think I am being insensitive to the depth of racism's pathology. Perhaps. But shouldn't it be debated? Are these ideas so dangerous that they should be censored? Bottom line, the dialogue is overdue. America needs a cathartic discussion on race and minority underperformance for the sake of our nation's future. Culture is no more immutable than poverty, discrimination, sexism, or any of the thousands of burdens that individuals overcome on a regular basis. The glory of America is that it allows people to rise beyond their backgrounds. But they must be honest in diagnosing and addressing their problems.

> The concept that "I can't succeed because I live in a racist society" has become as serious a problem to twenty-first-century America as racism itself.

Chapter One
Great Nations Need Great Citizens

A nation's wealth and status are like starlight: what you see is not what is, but what was. Just as the light we see from a distant star started its journey thousands of years ago, so is the nation's current success due principally to past actions. Great nations have great momentum; past investments in education and productivity continue to give benefits even after those good traits deteriorate. To a large degree, one generation benefits from the seeds planted by its fathers and mothers. We, in turn, plant seeds that will be reaped by our children. Some of these "seeds" are measurable; some are immeasurable. We do measure and lament that the Japanese are now investing twice as much as we are in new tools and equipment and that the Chinese are saving ten times more than we are. We know from educational scores that our children are in the bottom third in all international comparisons. We wring our hands over the yearly trade deficit. But *what* we measure is only a small part of our status.

The real strength of a nation is in those things we do not measure. These intangible assets also grow or decline. Herein lies the fate of empires. What drove seventh-century Arabs to organize themselves and burst out of their parched land, to handily defeat the Persian empire and almost capture Europe? Whoever would have guessed that these disorganized nomads would threaten anyone, let alone Europe? "Civilization was thrust into the brain of Europe on the point of a Moorish lance," observed Robert Ingersoll. What inspired the Mongols? Or the Greeks under Alexander? Often underequipped and half-starved, these nations and many others found an amazing bravery and initiative that took them to victory.

The key seems to be the spirit and attitude of their people. A nation's human resources are inevitably more important than its natural resources. Plato postulated in *The Republic* that the stability and success of a political community depend on the moral character of the people who make up that community. Alexis de Tocqueville observed that American democracy was largely based on the character and culture of the people, which was hard to quantify, but which ultimately would control the success or failure of the country. He warned that an excess of individualism would undercut the free institutions upon which democracy depended. Tocqueville called these positive habits and attitudes "habits of the heart." Professor Robert Bellah has used that phrase as a title of a book, in which he writes, "One of the keys to the survival of free institutions is the relationship between private and public life, the way in which citizens do, or do not, participate in the public sphere." Great nations cannot be judged by the success of their stock exchanges or their GNP; great nations have great intangibles, assets that can't be measured or quantified. Great nations must have great citizens, and the kind of future we will have depends on what kind of people we are and what kind of children we produce. One wise historian, Pasquale Villani, observed more than 400 years ago:

> Great nations must have great citizens, and the kind of future we will have depends on what kind of people we are and what kind of children we produce.

> To make a nation truly great, a handful of heroes capable of great deeds at supreme moments is not enough. Heroes are not always available, and one can often do without them! But it is essential to have thousands of reliable people—honest citizens—who steadfastly place the public interest before their own.

John Gardner, former secretary of Health, Education, and Welfare, similarly warns:

> Our society cannot achieve greatness unless individuals at many levels of ability accept the need for high standards of performance and strive to achieve those standards within the limits possible for them. We want the highest conceivable excellence, of course, in the activities crucial to our effectiveness and creativity as a society, but that isn't enough. If the man

in the street says, "Those fellows at the top have to be good, but I'm just a slob and can act like one."—Then our days of greatness are behind us.

Gardner noted that we need "excellence at every level in our society, excellent engineers and excellent first-grade teachers." Tocqueville marveled at the American trait of citizenship. He pointed out that there is an important difference between an inhabitant and a citizen, noting that for the inhabitant, "the condition of his village, the policing of his roads, and the repair of his church and parsonage do not concern him; he thinks that all of those things have nothing to do with him at all, but belong to a powerful stranger called the government."

Tocqueville concluded that when a nation loses the traits of citizenship (i.e., its public virtues), it perishes. There is hubris in America of late that God is an American who will watch over us no matter how inefficient and hedonistic we become. Democracy has triumphed, but our Constitution will not save us if the intangibles go sour. The Constitution is the framework, the structure for the checks and balances, for correction when human faction or folly moves us to excess. A ruthlessly ambitious person in one branch of government would rise up to find himself checkmated by the other parts of the system. The structure allows free men and women to live their lives, create wealth, and build their country.

Less mentioned but equally important to the success of our nation is the foundation upon which the

Constitution was built. Our founders assumed the often-unarticulated values, customs, mores, and culture of hardworking people who cared about the future. They assumed these public virtues would continue. Mary Ann Glendon, in her thoughtful book *Rights Talk*, points out that the founders of our country

> counted on families, custom, religion, and convention to preserve and promote the virtues required by our experiment in ordered liberty. Jefferson, Adams, and especially Madison knew that the Constitution and laws, the institutionalized checks on power, the army, and militia could not supply all the conditions required for the success of the new regime. They often explicitly acknowledged the dependence of the entire enterprise on the qualities of mind and character with which they believed the American population had been blessed.

If you change the underlying social milieu, not even the brilliance of the Constitution can save the country. The Constitution is a structure for citizens who are dedicated and motivated. It will not save a society that does not vote, does not have a strong civic life, has no sense of posterity, and is addicted to hedonism. The Constitution, however brilliant, will not make up for people who have lost the ability to care about the future of their nation.

America talks endlessly about the follies of its leaders, but what about the follies of its citizens? America in many respects faces more of a citizenship problem than a leadership problem. Ortega y Gasset found that "what makes a nation great is not primarily its great men, but the stature of its innumerable mediocre ones." Too many Americans believe that our nation has a divine destiny, but this is a dangerous hubris. As Arnold Toynbee warned, all great nations rise and all fall, and the "autopsy of history would show that all great nations commit suicide."

Every once-great nation in history thought God was on its side, but to date God has never allowed any great civilization to exist for very long. Greatness in nations is not a geopolitical status, but an ephemeral stage. We talk about "American exceptionalism," but we are merely whistling past history's graveyard, in which every other once-great civilization lies buried. It is time for a new reality in America. We are losing those stern virtues that made us a great nation in the first place and becoming an overindulged people with materialistic values that are not compatible with long-term greatness. We forget Roman satirist Juvenal's warning that "luxury is more ruthless than war." Americans know what they want, but not what they can afford. They have forgotten that rights and privileges require duties and responsibilities. We are today more threatened by a blanket of excess than by an iron curtain.

The battle flag that Admiral Nelson chose for the Battle of Trafalgar read "England expects every man to do his duty." Those words today seem an anachronism. We know all about our rights, but very little about our obligations. We speak of rights in a loud voice and responsibilities in a whisper. We want the fullest kinds of freedom in democracy, but unrestrained freedom may undercut democracy. Ambassador Henry Grunwald put it this way:

> We have not grasped the cost accounting of freedom. The great source of our current bafflement is that we somehow expect a wildly free society to have the stability of a tradition-guided society. (We somehow believe that we can simultaneously have, to the fullest, various kinds of freedoms: freedom from discipline, but also freedom from crime; freedom from community constraints, but also freedom from smog; freedom from economic controls, but also freedom from the inevitable ups and downs of a largely unhampered economy …) For freedom to be workable as a political and social system, strong inner controls, a powerful moral compass, and a sense of values are needed. In practice, the contradiction is vast. The compass is increasingly hard to read, the values hard to find in an open, mobile, fractioned society. Thus a troubling, paradoxical question: Does freedom destroy the inner disciplines that alone make freedom possible?

Democracy is built on an inordinate faith in ordinary people. Winston Churchill summed up democracy with the words "Trust the people." But, as Grunwald points out, that may be undercut if people lose their self-discipline and self-restraint. Freedom can thus be too free. "Freedom is the luxury of self-discipline," says one French philosopher. Well, we have the freedom, but little sign of self-discipline.

Having recently won the cold war, it is hard for Americans to take some of these warnings seriously. I would suggest we did not so much win the cold war as we outlasted the Soviets by borrowing from our children. We may decline right along with the Soviet Union. Saul Bellow states ominously, "The United States is as much threatened by an excess of liberty as Russia was from the absence of liberty."

To return to my earlier analogy, the seeds my generation planted and continues to plant will not keep our nation prosperous or stable. We are violating too many of the laws of economic gravity and social stability. Each one of us this year will get thousands of dollars more from government services than we are willing to pay for. It is not enough to say we do not want that much government—however much we democratically decide we want, we should pay for. We have hung an albatross of debt around our children's necks.

Our educational system's deterioration needs no elaboration. Read any morning newspaper. Thomas Jefferson stated, "If a nation expects to be ignorant and free ... it expects what never was and never will be." Fewer and fewer people read newspapers; fewer and fewer people even watch the network news. When asked what beliefs they would die for, 48 percent of participants in a large national poll said "none." Only 24 percent said they were willing to die for their country. Two-thirds of Americans have never given time to community activities or helped to solve community problems. Two-thirds of us cannot name our local congressperson. More than half believe they have no influence on the decisions made by local government. One-fourth admitted that they do not care about their neighborhood's problems. This is not compatible with greatness. We have ignored, or taken for granted, a vital building block necessary to continue greatness: some mutual sense of citizenship.

We can supply order for a while without citizenship, but not forever. We can ultimately never make enough laws or hire enough police to make up for a lack of self-discipline and self-restraint. A society that needs to put mesh fences over many of its freeway overpasses to keep fellow citizens from throwing harmful objects at each other does not seem to have lasting power. A society that talks seriously about granting "rights" to animals and trees but is silent about any obligations and responsibilities of citizenship lacks proportion and sustainability.

> There has been a great unbalancing in America. We have unbalanced community in favor of individualism, responsibilities in favor of rights, and duties in favor of privileges.

"Civilization begins with order, grows with liberty, and dies with chaos," warns Will Durant. We risk that outcome. There has been a great unbalancing in America. We have unbalanced community in favor of individualism, responsibilities in favor of rights, and duties in favor of privileges. We want education without study, wealth without work, freedom without participation, and democracy without citizenship. We must self-correct or perish, for this is hardly a sustainable agenda.

Chapter Two
The New Wealth of Nations

How important is culture in explaining the success or lack of success of various peoples? Anyone who travels in other countries cannot help but wonder why certain nations succeed brilliantly and other nations stumble along in poverty with marginal economies. The question hits an inquisitive person in the face as they travel and demand answers.

My wife and I spent six months traveling in South America in the 1960s, where we accepted the standard south-of-the-border excuse that the poverty and problems in South and Central America were caused by "Yankee Imperialism." It sounded logical and was reinforced by my (then) orthodox liberalism that had to find "victims" and "oppressors." The often-repeated complaint "Poor Mexico—so close to the United States, so far from God" spoke for all of South America. South America was a "victim" of a rapacious North America.

One can't help but wonder about the differences between North America and those nations south of the American border. South America and North America were roughly comparable in status in 1800, and many Europeans saw South America's future as much brighter than North America's. Latin America is amazingly rich in good land and natural resources. Latin American historian Claudio Véliz put it this way, "One group began poor, in the North, the other rich, in the South. In 500 years the positions have entirely reversed."

How true! South America is filled with political instability, economic chaos, and a standard of living that is only a fraction of that of North America. Corruption is a way of life, business, and government, and the discrepancy between rich and poor is almost unconscionable. Why have these talented people not been able to create wealth and sustain a decent standard of living?

Forty years ago, we assumed that the complaint that "Yankee Imperialism" caused the poverty of Latin America was too universal, too passionate not to contain truth. Likewise, in later travels, I found that Africans historically had, for all essential purposes, a single excuse for their poverty: colonialism. They would have been successful countries but for European domination. All of this was reinforced in my mind and theirs by the U.S. academic community and its liberal orthodoxy. The "dependency theory" is the standard academic explanation and teaches that many of the developing countries are being held back and oppressed by the developed countries, that *their* poverty can be largely explained by *our* wealth.

But time and experience made me at first skeptical, then antagonistic to these explanations. I was greatly influenced by reading Larry Harrison's powerful book *Underdevelopment Is a State of Mind*, in which he brilliantly compares Argentina with Australia, Haiti with Barbados, and Nicaragua with Costa Rica. He postulates that failure in these countries is "homegrown, and not the fault of others." Harrison went to Latin America with the U.S. Agency for International Development (AID). He acknowledges that economic development is a mix of many factors, but his thesis is that the single most important one—culture—is rarely discussed. Harrison's Typology of Progress-Prone and Progress-Resistant Cultures is found in Appendix A.

Harrison looks at Argentina and Australia and asks, "Why did Australia become so much more prosperous?" Both are very large countries with rich natural resources. Both have a largely European population. Yet Australia is a stable democracy with four times the per capita GNP of Argentina. As one Argentine states, "The basically passive, apathetic value orientation profile of the Argentine society must be regarded as the critical factor limiting the possibilities of steady, long-run economic development."

Spain was a flawed colonizing nation. It came to conquer, exploit, and convert. It looked at the New World as wealth to be harvested and taken back to Spain. Everywhere that Spain settled, it left crippled cultures in its wake. The results are still with us today, both in the nations of South and Central America and in those who emigrate from there.

A new equation is slowly emerging that helps explain the wealth of nations, a theory that emphasizes the culture, attitudes, beliefs, and values of the people of each nation. Classic economic development theory looked at many factors in examining national power, but emphasized the presence of natural resources. A country without iron ore, coal, oil, or substantial amounts of other natural resources could not become a modern economic power. A dated but classic economic study on Italy showed that while Rome once ruled the globe, in the modern economic world Italy did not have sufficient natural resources to become a major industrial power. By extension (though not covered in the study), Japan, Taiwan, and Hong Kong could never become major economic players. Wealth, when it was not plundered from someone else, was homegrown and created largely out of indigenous natural resources.

> A new equation is slowly emerging that helps explain the wealth of nations, a theory that emphasizes the culture, attitudes, beliefs, and values of the people of each nation. ... Japan, Singapore, South Korea, Taiwan, Hong Kong, and others have shown us that it is human resources that play the greatest role in economic development, not natural resources.

But Japan, Singapore, South Korea, Taiwan, Hong Kong, and others have shown us that it is human resources that play the greatest role in economic development, not natural resources. Nations poor in natural resources can substitute human resources for coal and iron ore and still become wealthy and prosperous. Renewable human skills are more important than the one-time inheritance of natural resources. As James Fallows observed, "It seems to me that the prospects for the Philippines are about as dismal as those for, say, South Korea are bright. In each case, the basic explanation seems to be culture: in one case a culture that brings out the productive best in the Koreans (or the Japanese, or now even the Thais) and in the other a culture that pulls many Filipinos toward their most self-destructive, self-defeating worst."

These new industrial models often import raw materials thousands of miles across oceans, turn them into goods and products, and ship them back to the source of the natural resources where they are sold at a profit. "Adding value" to natural resources is much more profitable than producing the natural resources in the first place.

This new equation does not argue that human resources are everything. Obviously, a collectivist system or totalitarian government can squelch even a skilled and motivated workforce. North Korea's poverty flows from a flawed economic and political system; change those factors and I suggest North Korea will do well. East Germany differed from West Germany because of a dysfunctional political and economic system. But note that even Communism could not completely suppress German industriousness before reunification. East Germany had the most prosperous economy in the eastern bloc. China and Taiwan share the same cultural traits, but only in the last twenty-five years has China partly overcome the stultifying drag of their political system.

A handful of countries have such rich reserves of natural resources that they are wealthy by inheritance.

Saudi Arabia, Kuwait, and the United Arab Emirates did not earn or create their wealth. They inherited it. Their experience has little applicability elsewhere.

In the nontotalitarian world, I suggest that Larry Harrison has correctly articulated the underdiscussed and underrated factors in determining the success of nations: culture, values, and attitudes. A person's (or nation's) beliefs and assumptions can account for their success or failure. Harrison is not alone. James Fallows, in his book *More Like Us*, observes, "In the long run, habits, values, and behavior of ordinary people determine national strength." Senator Patrick Moynihan similarly states, "The central conservative truth is that it is culture, not politics, that determines the success of a society." The more I observe the world, the more these words make sense to me.

Defining Culture and Seeing It in Action.

How do I use the word "culture"? Let us use the classic definition of Sir Edward Burnett Tylor, the founder of modern anthropology: "Culture … is that complex whole which includes knowledge, belief, art, morals, law, custom and any other capabilities and habits acquired by man as a member of society." Culture is thus the "learned" behavior that we acquire as a member of a society.

Economic development does not take place in a vacuum. Human beings are creatures whose behavior is molded by culture, customs, and the institutions built by the culture into which they are born. "We build our buildings," said Winston Churchill, "then they build us." Exactly! Culture is difficult to discuss in academic circles because it offends the liberal orthodoxy. Attacking a people's culture is thought to be as bad as attacking their race. We buy into "cultural relativism," in which all cultures are assumed to be equal. I suggest that all cultures deserve respect and understanding, but they are not all equal. Culture helps explain the success of Jews and Japanese, and it also helps explain the Hispanic drop-out rate. We should not be intimidated from discussing the obvious.

An important part of modern African culture is blaming all problems on colonialism. But there are the important issues that should be discussed instead of colonialism—for example, that we are not being fair to Africa in our trade policy, and we may well want to forgive many of the loans that are breaking the backs of Africa. Listen to what Ethiopian Prime Minister Meles Zenawi has said recently: "I think it is time for Africans to stop blaming everyone except themselves for the dire situation we find ourselves in. We need to own up to our own shortcoming in the past and come up with alternative strategies and implement them." Ironically, there is some evidence that the African countries that received the most foreign aid are the most dysfunctional. Good-hearted generosity often ends up making problems worse.

We are making too many excuses for failure. It is not doing Africa a favor to reinforce the concept that the legacy of colonialism is holding it back. It is internal factors that the Africans must concentrate upon, not merely external factors. Tribalism in Africa better explains Africa's dilemma than colonialism, though the roots of poverty and wealth are multidimensional. But we do a grave injustice to our friends when we reinforce their excuses. Nations, like individuals, love to blame others for their faults. It's a human response. I believe, however, that dysfunctional nations will not get better until they admit the real nature of their problems and take responsibility for their own weaknesses.

> Nations, like individuals, love to blame others for their faults. It's a human response. I believe, however, that dysfunctional nations will not get better until they admit the real nature of their problems and take responsibility for their own weaknesses.

Colonialism is more of an excuse than an explanation. It excuses much; it explains little. If colonialism is to be blamed for most of Africa's ills, we should observe a similar impact wherever colonialism has put down roots. If colonialism is a "dependent variable," then it must leave its nasty legacy wherever it has existed. Yet many countries have treated colonialism as a hurdle, not a barrier. They made use of the advantages of colonialism and were not defeated by the negatives.

European colonialism in Africa interrupted and disrupted traditional African societies; it exploited and divided tribes. In certain cases, such as with Portugal and Belgium, the colonizing countries were particularly brutal and cruel to the local people. Nowhere was colonialism without its abuses. On the other hand, colonialism also left Africa with incredible assets, including better health, education, literacy, infrastructure, and whole economies that were developed by the colonialists and passed on to the newly independent nations. European colonialism in Africa was nowhere as harsh as Japanese and Chinese colonialism was in Korea. In Africa, colonialism lasted sixty years, in Korea, hundreds of years, yet South Korea left colonialism behind and has prospered.

Korea's per capita GNP in 1961 stood at $82 (U.S.)—near the bottom of the international income scale. "It had all the problems of a resource poor, low-income developing country with the bulk of its population dependent on scarce farmland for bare subsistence," according to one standard guidebook. Today, Korea is universally recognized as an economic miracle. Why? Some say because the United States gave foreign aid. That's true, but it is of small importance. Korea's success is widely written about. Nowhere do I detect but passing mention of foreign aid being a principal or even an important factor. South Korea created its wealth; it helped itself far more than it was helped by others.

Africa has actually received far more foreign aid than Korea (in total dollars, not per capita), but Africa has little to show for it. Between 1960 and the present, hundreds of billions have been given to sub-Saharan Africa. But as African writer Hilary Ng Wengo states in *Plundered Eden*, "[Leaders in Africa] mismanaged economies, squandered national wealth and literally threw away the future of their people as they jostled with one another for personal power and gain."

Similar stories abound in other colonies and former colonies. Hong Kong was a colony, and yet it produces more wealth than Zaire, Zimbabwe, Zambia, Malawi, Tanzania, Angola, Mozambique, and Botswana combined—despite the fact that Hong Kong has no natural resources and the above-named African countries are generally rich in them. Hong Kong does have a culture that stresses hard work, skills, and motivation. Singapore is a former British colony (like Kenya), and it had a colonial government longer than any in Africa. Today it is one of the most prosperous countries in the world. Singapore took what the British had left, added a rich culture that stressed education, and achieved meteoric success. Barbados is a former British colony peopled by the descendants of slaves who were uprooted from Africa and brought under unspeakable conditions to the New World. Yet 257,000 Barbados citizens create more wealth on 166 square miles than "Free and Independent" Liberia does with ten times as many people and no legacy of colonialism. Barbados adopted British culture and values.

Colonialism, therefore, is not the dependent variable that influences the success or failure of countries. It has not held back societies and cultures that had the ability and willingness to overcome the negatives and accentuate the positives. This is not to justify colonialism, only to accept it as a historical fact and seek to evaluate its consequences. Colonialism happened. The question that must be asked is, Are these countries better or worse off because of the colonial experience?

Worldwide, colonialism has left very mixed results. Does it do much to explain Africa's current problems? I am very skeptical. It may have had a larger impact on Mozambique and Zaire because they had a more brutal experience with it, but I doubt that it explains anywhere near as much as its proponents claim.

We must, above all, be honest and candid in our evaluations of the success or failure of each individual culture. Better a brutal truth than a well-meaning lie. Increasingly, Africans are rejecting the excuse of colonialism. Ali A. Mazrui, in his book *Cultural Forces in World Politics*, argues that African culture has taken the wrong things from the West:

> We borrowed the profit motive, but not the entrepreneurial spirit. We borrowed the acquisitive appetites of capitalism, but not the creative risk taking. We are at home with Western gadgets, but are bewildered by Western workshops. We wear the wristwatches, but refuse to watch [them] for the culture of punctuality. We have learned to parade in display, but not to drill in discipline. The West's consumption patterns have arrived, but not necessarily the West's technique of production.

We owe our international neighbors our honest diagnosis. I believe that in the non-Communist world, most countries have their present and future in their own hands and have mostly themselves to blame for their deficiencies. South America is not poor because the United States is exploiting it (though we clearly have done that to some extent); it is poor because the people have what James Fallows calls a "damaged culture." Tough words, I admit, but confirmed by the South Americans themselves. Larry Harrison dedicates one of his books to Carlos Rangel, a Venezuelan journalist, and quotes him: "It was Latin America's destiny to be colonized by a country that, though admirable in many ways, was at the time beginning to reject the emerging spirit of modernism, and to build walls against the rise of rationalism, empiricism, and free thought—that is to say, against the very basis of the modern industrial and liberal revolution, and of capitalist economic development."

Rangel blames not colonialism for Latin America's problems, but "antisocial individualism, an adversity to work and an affinity for violence and authoritarianism." If your religion (your culture) teaches that if you rise above your status you risk your soul and your status in your next life, your society will have less social mobility. You may well find more peace in such a society, and you likely will develop fewer ulcers, but it is counterproductive to what the developed world thinks of as human progress. It limits not only wealth and motivation, but individual creative capacity, literacy rates, and life expectancy. It is hard to write off these social accomplishments as merely "Western materialism." Good health, low infant mortality, the ability to reach one's potential and to advance one's talents seem to become important to all advanced societies.

The principal variable that separates the success of Hong Kong and Taiwan from the poverty of Brazil and Kenya is culture. The values, attitudes, and beliefs that people bring to a particular experience are of overwhelming importance. This, then, is the growing consensus: those cultures that stress education, delayed gratification, hard work, the acquisition of skills, and so on have an incredible advantage over those that do not. Those countries and cultures that have built institutions that recognize merit in advancement (what you know, rather than who you know), political stability, and that instill in their people a desire for education and self-betterment are the countries that have succeeded in the new international marketplace. Success and performance are closely linked to attitudes and values. Understand the difference in attitudes and values, and you will much better understand the difference in performance.

> We are all God's children, and every person and every culture deserves understanding and respect. But as we search for why some have a high standard of living and others a low one, we must not avoid the examination of the cultural differences between societies.

We are all God's children, and every person and every culture deserves understanding and respect. But as we search for why some have a high standard of living and others a low one, we must not avoid the examination of the cultural differences between societies. No matter how "controversial." For when we ask why some countries and some peoples live in poverty and squalor and others in prosperity, we all must look in the mirror for the most important factor. This also applies to our American counterparts, blacks and Hispanics. We cannot continue to tolerate without dissent the excuse of "systemic racial oppression" by the white community. Once South America and Africa stopped blaming others and started to take responsibility for their own ills, the healing process accelerated. This seems to apply to American blacks and Hispanics. Some of their spokespersons are beginning the process, but they will have to own more of their own problems to fully take their place in American society. They will then be the authors of their own salvation.

Chapter Three
Two Paths

One of the major issues facing America's minority communities is what should be their post–civil rights strategy.
I should like to describe two contrasting paths that I
believe lie before the leaders of the minority community.
In the 1950s, the English writer C. P. Snow's published
an immensely influential essay titled "Two Cultures" in
which he compared the world of science with the world
of arts and literature. For fifty years, this article was a
major influence in science policy and public policy.

Some will object and say that, C. P. Snow notwithstanding, "two paths" is too polarizing and simplistic a
metaphor. There are always more than two alternatives,
more than two wands, more than two cultures, and
more than two paths, and of course those critics are
right. There *are* more than two.

Yet we should not fail to see the use and power of
stark contrast. Contrasting alternatives is important,
not in planning actual strategies, but to simplify complex issues, highlight differences, and to illuminate the
larger issues. The path of the last fifty years in attacking
racism was legislation and group pressure. It worked
brilliantly. But now I believe that minorities are not

going to achieve the American dream without a new emphasis on self-improvement, self-advancement, and self-discipline. That is not to say we should stop fighting racism. Fighting racism surely should be built into our society's DNA. The Urban Institute recently conducted a study in which blacks and whites with identical resumes applied for identical jobs, only to find that black males were three times as likely to be rejected as white males. Whites in this and other studies are hired more often and offered higher salaries. I do not contend that this phase of the battle is over. But I believe a new emphasis on minority self-reliance is needed, indeed is overdue. Notwithstanding discrimination, we are making too many excuses for minority underperformance.

> I believe that minorities are not going to achieve the American dream without a new emphasis on self-improvement, self-advancement, and self-discipline. That is not to say we should stop fighting racism. Fighting racism surely should be built into our society's DNA.

Black high school graduates with similar test scores to whites are earning 87 percent of white wages. Still unfair, but within striking distance. Blacks are clearly better positioned to move to success than the Jews of the early twentieth century, who faced even greater barriers than minorities do today. The Italians in the twentieth century closed a much larger gap through hard work and determination.

The gap between black and white earnings and

performance would seem almost bridgeable by adjusting black attitudes toward education. Laurence Steinberg notes in *Beyond the Classroom* that black students do not work as hard in school as similarly situated whites, they watch more TV, do less homework, spend less time on task, and come to class much less prepared. Correcting these factors does not need a governmental program, but it does need self-correction by those involved.

So let us stipulate that we should always strongly enforce our civil rights laws and stand firm against racism. But that can't be the entire battle plan. To put such a total emphasis on the evils of racism can have unintended consequences. It ignores fifty years of social revolution that has moved massive numbers of blacks into the middle class. Telling people that they are victims can be limiting, enervating, and self-defeating, even if they are victims. It can lead to powerlessness and defeatism. It can make worse the problem we are trying to solve.

Compare two alternative paths to a better, more successful life for American minorities. One path lies in putting the main effort into "group rights" and fighting for new civil rights laws, reparations, and new forms and varieties of affirmative action. Down this path, it is the larger society that must correct itself. The second path would put the main efforts into minority self-improvement. It would stress that minorities' success lies mainly in their own hands and efforts. This path would emphasize education, persuading minority youth to finish school, avoiding out-of-wedlock births, and helping minorities gain the skills and traits needed by the marketplace for self-advancement. It would identify the black community itself as the main source of economic and social advancement. Minorities would stop looking for what African American professor Shelby Steele (whose metaphor I borrow) calls "salvation by society" and force them to look more to their own inner resources.

These are very different paths, which lead to very different consequences. The first path leads to concentrating on civil rights, group rights, litigation, political pressure, claims for reparations, and the endless reliance of the grievance industry. I do not mean to be pejorative, for this first path was appropriate for the last fifty years. But it is not the path for the next fifty years. The second path continues to demand equal rights under the law, but teaches children that the road to success is through education, self-advancement, and hard work, and that the American dream is available to all. It would not teach children that they are victims, but instead that they are the beneficiaries of a great liberation movement. The first path stresses dependency on government and collective pressure on the political system. The second path stresses self-improvement. Although not mutually exclusive, these are very different options.

The first path was the strategic and necessary path during the last half of the last century. America did have blatant discrimination and significant racial barriers. American minorities age fifty and older were born into a world where, in many parts of America, the barriers were practically insurmountable, no matter the individual's education and personal effort. No part of America gave minorities full equal rights and opportunities, though some geographic areas were better than others. But that world has dramatically changed. America's conversion to equal rights and social justice has been one of the great revolutions of world history. Martin Luther King Jr. stands with Gandhi in the pantheon of heroes of social justice. A black or Hispanic baby born today is born into a world transformed—not a perfect world, but a world that is closer to a meritocracy than at any point in human history. Yes, racism and discrimination exist, but less so now than at any other point in human history. Heaven on earth? No, not close. Yet we live in a reasonably just and fair society that allows social and economic mobility.

> A black or Hispanic baby born today is born into a world transformed—not a perfect world, but a world that is closer to a meritocracy than at any point in human history.

I sense that the new interest in the black community in reparations and a new emphasis in the Hispanic community in bilingualism and defending illegal immigration have a powerful capacity to create antagonism with the white community that could produce a significant backlash. White America only accepts partial responsibility for minority underperformance and feels that the playing field is now roughly level. Additionally, there is a new but often unexpressed feeling among minority leaders that the emphasis should shift more to self-development. TV dad and comedian Bill Cosby has strongly criticized low-income African Americans for "not holding up their end of the deal" and urges them to take more responsibility for their families and communities. He postulates that blacks can have no real power without taking responsibility for their own education and economic development. Similarly, black scholar Glen Lowery put it brilliantly:

> It is now beyond dispute that many of the problems of contemporary black American life lie outside the reach of effective governmental action and require for their successful resolution actions that can only be undertaken by the black community itself. These problems involve at their core the values, attitudes and behaviors of individual blacks. Too much of the political energy, talent and imagination abounding in the emerging black middle class is being channeled into a struggle against an "enemy without" while the "enemy within" goes relatively unchecked.

Lionel Sosa makes a similar point in the book *The Americano Dream* when he says to the Hispanic community, "Remember, our Spanish conquerors, for their own benefit, deliberately created an oppressed underclass whose collective psyche became rooted in pacificity and underachievement. We must free ourselves of these cultural shackles, for they exist, all right, but only in our minds."

The battles for social justice have *not* been entirely won, but today the path lies more in fighting for economic justice for all and less along racial divides. History teaches that large discrepancies in wealth are destabilizing and can even cause revolutions if extreme enough. A few people in America are getting too much of the economic pie. These battles transcend race and address the issues inherent in the next turn of history's wheel. They are issues that concern whites, blacks, and Hispanics, and to win these battles, we should be united as Americans rather than being divided by race.

> **Never in human history have people of color had as much opportunity for economic and social advancement as America in the twenty-first century.**

We should not abandon our efforts to eliminate discrimination or change America into a color-blind society through public policy. It is time to begin the transition from minorities as victims to a new emphasis on minorities as victors; it is time to move from group empowerment to self-empowerment. Never in human history have people of color had as much opportunity for economic and social advancement as America in the twenty-first century. But their fate lies largely in their own hands.

Chapter Four

Are Mexicans Italians? Are Blacks Africans?

One of the most important questions facing America and the Southwest is, Are Mexicans Italians? Italians were one of the last immigrant groups to come to America under antagonism and suspicion. Prejudice was palpable, discrimination widespread, intergroup relations difficult. Italians 100 years ago, like Mexican immigrants today, had poor graduation rates, high drop-out rates, higher crime rates, fewer college graduates per capita, and fewer professionals than other whites. It seemed for a time that Italians would be a permanent underclass of blue-collar workers.

But Italians, while they took longer to succeed in traditional ways, took on the educational and success patterns of the majority community, and now they equal or exceed the performance of the majority community. They are among the proudest Americans, with family income and professional status higher than the national average. Are Mexicans Italians?

Samuel P. Huntington, who gave us the perceptive *The Clash of Civilizations and the Remaking of World Order*, has a new book, *Who Are We?*, which should be much debated by those who care about Americans' future. Huntington worries that "The persistent inflow of Hispanic immigrants threatens to divide the United States into two peoples, two cultures, and two languages." He makes a powerful case that Mexicans and other Latinos might not assimilate into mainstream U.S. culture, partly because such a disproportionate part of our immigrant stream are Hispanics (forming instead their own political and linguistic enclaves—from Los Angeles to Miami—and rejecting the Anglo-Protestant values that built the American dream). As he states, "The United States ignores this challenge at its peril."

All American history is opposed to Huntington's thesis and is on the side of success of our new immigrants. America has been a powerful assimilating machine, and every immigrant group has had its doubting xenophobes and mean-spirited skeptics. I mean to be neither, nor do I think Huntington is. Hispanic Americans have fought and died for America in impressive numbers and, as a proportion of their numbers, have won more Medals of Honor for bravery than any group in America. But there are three big differences distinguishing current immigration patterns that make nonassimilation an equally likely scenario. Huntington distinguishes today's immigrants from historic immigrants by pointing out three distinct factors; all begin with "D."

> **Distance:** Previous generations of immigrants had to come a long way and didn't have much option to go home. They had to totally throw themselves into becoming Americans. Today

many of our immigrants can go back to their homes for a weekend. The pull to assimilate is considerably less. With dual citizenship, they vote both for president of Mexico and the United States.

Diversity: The only way past immigrants could talk to their neighbors and live their lives was to learn English and assimilate. But no longer. Never in history has America accepted so disproportionate a percentage of one nationality and language group. (See Huntington's chart.) Today over 50 percent of our immigrants are Spanish speaking, and America is backing into becoming a bilingual/bicultural country. I know of no bilingual/bicultural country in the world that lives at peace with itself.

> Today over 50 percent of our immigrants are Spanish speaking, and America is backing into becoming a bilingual/bicultural country. I know of no bilingual/bicultural country in the world that lives at peace with itself.

Discontinuity: The history of American immigration shows times of large immigration followed by periods of low immigration (due to war, depression, and other factors), which give the new immigrants a chance to assimilate and join our community. Today we annually take approximately 1 million legal immigrants and have 9 to 11 million illegal immigrants residing here, with massive numbers of illegals being added year after year. There is never the pause that assimilates. Will the melting pot becoming a pressure cooker?

Why not take into account in our immigration policy the skills of potential immigrants, like all other immigrant-receiving countries do? Isn't it irreverent that the average Asian immigrant arrives with 14.5 years of education, while the average Mexican immigrant arrives with 7.6 years? Isn't it relevant that the drop-out rate of Hispanic students approaches 50 percent? Are we really that confident in the ability of America to turn all immigrants into productive citizens? Or is it hubris?

Too many of our Mexican immigrants live in ethnic ghettos. Too many are unskilled laborers, too many are uneducated, too many live in poverty, too many are illegal, too many haven't finished ninth grade, too many drop out of school. Too many don't have health insurance and too many go on welfare. The question has to be asked: Are we laying the foundations for a new, Hispanic underclass?

The National Center for Education Statistics (2001) finds about 28 percent of Latino adolescents drop out of high school, far in excess of the 13 percent of African American adolescents and 7 percent of Caucasian adolescents. Even more disturbing, the RAND Corporation in their study "Immigration in a

Changing Economy—California's Experience" found that the initial earnings of Japanese, Korean, and Chinese immigrants were 76 percent of the native average; ten years later, they had risen to 103 percent of the native average. However, Mexicans, California's largest immigrant stream, started at 52 percent of the native average and *declined* to 47 percent ten years later.

Let me quote one study regarding what is happening all over America:

> Ethnic ghettoization and its retardation of assimilation are more serious now than a hundred years ago. At that time only rarely did a single ethnic group dominate an area of several city blocks and even then many immigrants moved out of such areas. Now ethnic enclaves are huge and growing; in the city of Miami, for example, fifty percent of the population speaks English poorly or not at all, and seventy-three percent speak a language other than English at home.

Robert J. Samuelson, writing about Mexican immigration in *The Washington Post*, states:

> Our interest lies in less immigration from Mexico, while Mexico's interest lies in more. The United States has long been an economic safety value for Mexico: a source of jobs for its poor. The same desperate forces that drive people north mean that once they get here

they face long odds in joining the American economic and social mainstream.

He goes on to say:

Surely we don't need more poor and unskilled workers, and Mexican immigrants fall largely into this category. The stakes here transcend economics. Americans are unjustly proud of being a nation of immigrants ... (But) ... many Mexican immigrants have little desire to join the American mainstream precisely because their overriding motive for coming was economic and their homeland is so close. Their primary affection remains with Mexico.

Melting pots that don't melt become pressure cookers. Diversity carried too far is divisiveness. Whatever we decide on the immigration numbers, we must take great care to avoid becoming a Hispanic Quebec.

I am skeptical of mass immigration because I believe that America should stabilize its population and move from growth to sustainability. But whatever we do, immigrants must be assimilated and acculturated into our melting pot and incorporated into our economy. As an example of a

> [W]hatever we do, immigrants must be assimilated and acculturated into our melting pot and incorporated into our economy.

successful assimilation, African immigrants do amazingly well in the United States and clearly can serve as role models to African Americans. An incredible percentage of Harvard graduates are from either Africa or the West Indies, areas that have not been corrupted by the cult of victimhood.

There is an orthodox liberalism that prevents us from honestly debating these sensitive issues of race, language, and culture. We can't solve problems that we don't talk about. We are growing a Hispanic Quebec in America, a nation within a nation, and we are doing so without adequate debate or discussion.

From Diversity to Dominance
Foreign-Born Population Living in the United States

1960
In 1960, the foreign-born population in the United States (from the five principal countries of origin) was relatively diverse:

2000
In 2000, the foreign-born population from the top five countries was distributed very differently:

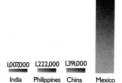

7,841,000

748,000	833,000	953,000	990,000	1,257,000	952,000	1,007,000	1,222,000	1,391,000	
Poland	U.K.	Canada	Germany	Italy	Cuba	India	Philippines	China	Mexico

Source: Campbell J. Gibson and Emily Lennon's "Historical Census Statistics on the Foreign-Born Population of the United States 1850–1990" (Population Division Working Paper No. 29, U.S. Census Bureau, February 1999); and "Profile of the Foreign-Born Population in the United States: 2000" (Washington: U.S. Census Bureau, Current Population Reports, series p. 23–206, 201).

Chapter Five

Honor Diversity, but Celebrate Unity

The same liberal orthodoxy that keeps us from honestly discussing minority underperformance demands that we "celebrate diversity." If a little diversity is good, a lot of diversity will be better, until we live in a giant multicultural United Nations. We do not honor the success of the melting pot anymore. We now are told to see ourselves as a salad bowl or mosaic where we all maintain our own cultures and language. Multiculturalism reigns.

> Too many Americans believe that we have a divine destiny and that God will watch over us no matter how diverse we become or how hedonistic, selfish, myopic, or inefficient we become. This is a dangerous hubris.

But one can fairly ask, Where is the working model? Where in history or in today's globe do different people with different languages and different cultures live together in peace? We cast ourselves adrift from our historic model at some risk to our stability and tranquility. What is necessary to maintain community? Too many Americans believe that we have a divine destiny and that God will watch over us no matter how diverse we become or how hedonistic, selfish, myopic, or inefficient we become. This is a dangerous hubris.

A community is much more than a place on a map. It is a state of mind, shared values, shared vision, a common fate. A diverse community is not a state of nature. A herd is a state of nature, a flock, a covey, a gaggle are states of nature, but alas, not a community. A community of different religions, races, and nationalities is against most of the lessons of history, as we see daily on our TV sets. Humans bond to families, but not necessarily with their neighbors. A community requires a unique set of skills: social architects, bridge builders, and structural engineers who build bonds and bridges, who remove barriers between people. Community needs shared customs, traditions, values, principles, and institutions.

> A community is not geography; it is not *who* lives in an area, but the web of human relationships of the people who live in a particular place.

The United States is by definition a place on the map, but it is not intrinsically a community. A community is not geography; it is not *who* lives in an area, but the web of human relationships of the people who live in a particular place. As every house is not a home, every spot on the map is not a community. Houses shelter, homes nurture. Communities nurture. Communities are forged by commitment, dedication, hard work, tolerance, love, and a search for commonalties. Our forefathers and foremothers built a community and passed it onto us, but it is not like the Mississippi River or Mount McKinley, which we will inevitably pass on to our children. We will not inevitably pass community to our children. Community is not a guarantee; it is a continuing challenge.

Americans are endlessly citing the nineteenth-century Frenchman Alexis de Tocqueville (as I have) on his positive observations on America. But note that, bottom line, Tocqueville was skeptical of the American model lasting: "I would like to contribute to the faith in human perfectibility. But until men have changed their nature and are completely transformed, I will refuse to believe in the longevity of a government whose task is to hold together forty diverse peoples spread across a surface equal to half of Europe, to keep them from falling into rivalries, plots, and struggles, and to bring together their independent wills into action for common plans."

> Successful communities, successful countries don't just happen. They are built by dedication, sacrifice, and hard work. They must find or build unifying bonds and values. They also are built by caring for each other, helping each other, and working jointly on projects and programs.

We cannot rely on past success to insure future success, and we cannot take the future for granted. Successful communities, successful countries don't just happen. They are built by dedication, sacrifice, and hard work. They must find or build unifying bonds and values. They also are built by caring for each other, helping each other, and working jointly on projects and programs.

Our parents left us freedom, but more than that, we were left an equilibrium between freedom and order—a first-rate infrastructure, small national debt, and a tradition of barn raising and tolerance. They left us with a diverse people forged into one nation. And America has to date made diversity work. But we are testing its limits. What are the institutional structures and traits that promote stable communities? How do we achieve unity with diversity? What is the web of relationships and comity that make up a successful community?

A Community Will Remain a Community only as Long as It Has Justice and Honors Peaceful Changes.

There is nothing more important to community than justice. People must feel that they are fairly treated and that when justice is administered, it is evenhanded and proportionate. If I don't spend a lot of time recounting the reasons justice is needed, it is not that it isn't important, but that it is obvious. You simply can't have community without justice.

A Community Must Generate Tolerance and Yet Set Limits on That Tolerance. It Must Balance Freedom with Social Order, Rights with Responsibilities, Autonomy with Community.

One of the chief challenges of a community of diverse people is deciding what it should tolerate and what it should not tolerate. "Tolerance" is a word easy to say but hard to apply. History shows that diverse people need freedom of religion. It is your right to read your Bible, your Koran, your Torah, and believe what you will. It is *not* your right to force these readings on others. The American community tolerates almost any idea and religion, and a community should be alive with argument.

But the standards for teaching and tolerance are not coterminous. What does a diverse community teach its children in school? It may be that you deeply believe that trees moving make the wind blow. This is your prerogative, and you can teach it to your children, but you cannot teach it to my children in public institutions. You can stage debates in your school between Republicans and Democrats, because their differences are a subject open to debate and constantly changing, but you cannot give equal time in schools to how trees moving makes the wind blow. Science and rational thought have put to rest certain arguments, and knowledge must move forward if we are to survive in a competitive world. We can tolerate many private beliefs, but we should stand strong against institutionalizing non-science and scientific error into our school system.

There are some people who believe the Holocaust never happened. They are entitled to be mistaken, even gravely mistaken. They can stand on a soapbox on Main Street and profess that there was no Holocaust. But they cannot teach in our schools a viewpoint that all evidence points against. We have pictures of concentration camps and Holocaust victims. And we have pictures in rocks called fossils that show us the inspiring story of evolution. Schools must struggle with knowledge, but they cannot teach a particular theology or all minority viewpoints, no matter how passionately held.

Should our schools teach about democracy and freedom? It is hard to argue with Diane Ravitch, a thoughtful educational expert, who writes, "I suggest that what our schools must do is to teach young people the virtues and blessings of our democratic system of government. If we value our rights and freedoms, we must understand how we got them and what it would mean to live in a society that did not have them."

The public schools have been the great melting pot and the conveyer of American history and civic pride. "For many generations of immigrants, the common school was the primary teacher of patriotism and civic values," observes Ravitch, who points out that too many school systems are teaching students to identify with their race or their ethnic or cultural origins rather than with the overarching civic ideals of the American community. We do so at the risk to our stability. The public school system must teach some level of civic values and the traits of citizenship.

Even more important is tolerance in the area of behavior, especially where behavior does not hurt others, and/or where no societal

> [T]oo many school systems are teaching students to identify with their race or their ethnic or cultural origins rather than with the overarching civic ideals of the American community.

consensus exists. What should a community made up of various races, religions, and ethnic groups tolerate, and what should it not tolerate? The late Barbara Jordan talked about the need to "Americanize" immigrants. How tolerant should our society be and what should we demand of immigrants from other cultures who come here with vastly different ideas of individualism, constitutionalism, human rights, equality, liberty, rule of law, democracy, separation of church and state, and private property? How many conflicting, contrasting, and overlapping cultures can live together in peace and harmony? What happens when a separatist cultures clashes with a pluralist culture, when "Why can't we all just get along?" meets "There is no God but Allah"?

Certainly there should be freedom of religion, but can people handle snakes, refuse medical care, and refuse on religious grounds to salute the flag? People can refuse a blood transfusion for themselves and even all medical care if they want. We have generally allowed people to do these things on grounds of their religion. But should they be allowed to refuse medical care for their minor children? Can they force their thirteen-year-old daughter to marry her forty-five-year-old uncle or submit to female genital mutilation? Should Muslim clerics have the right to broadcast over outdoor loudspeakers the five daily Islamic calls to prayer? Should we give in to demands of some Muslim clerics for publicly maintained prayer facilities in such institutions as schools and airports? Should a Muslim woman be able to get her driver's license picture taken while in purdah?

Does the state have to maintain kosher kitchens in its prison system? Can Hispanic students demand a separate graduation where the Mexican, not the

American flag is flown? Should the ritual slaughter of animals be forbidden under our animal rights laws? Do we grant a zoning variance to allow a mosque to build a prayer tower? Should Sikhs be allowed to wear their daggers, so central to their religion, on airplanes? Louisiana cockfighters are suing the federal government over a new ban on shipping fighting birds, saying it's discrimination against Cajuns and Hispanics. They claim that the ban is "moral imperialism" and that cockfighting is integral to their culture. All of these examples challenge us to think about the limits to tolerance and multiculturalism.

Certainly there can and should be some reasonable accommodation to diversity. Can someone in our public hospitals refuse to be treated by a black or Jewish doctor? We say no, absolutely not! But how about our Muslim immigrants whose religion forbids another man from seeing or touching the body of a married (or single) woman? Why not allow her request for a woman doctor for reasons of public health? Yet we are not going to let her perform female genital mutilation on her twelve-year-old daughter. Finding a balance between tolerance and chaos, rights and privileges, freedom and community will always be a work in progress. To resolve these questions, we shall need honest and candid discussions that are not hampered by political correctness.

> Finding a balance between tolerance and chaos, rights and privileges, freedom and community will always be a work in progress.

A Community Can Be a Joseph's Coat of Many Colors and Creeds, but It Must Have More Things in Common Than Differences. It Must Stress the *Unum*, Not the *Pluribus*.

I enjoy the vast number of different races and nationalities that make up America. It is appropriate to celebrate diversity, but I suggest we must celebrate unity even more. In my travels around the world, I have seen no place, with the possible exception of the United States, where "diversity" is working. Diverse people worldwide are often engaged in hating each other—that is, when they are not killing each other. A diverse peaceful or stable society is against most historical precedent. It cannot be achieved with slogans or happy talk. It is much harder to achieve than most Americans acknowledge. A nation is not a rooming house where we all live separately while we share the same space. I believe that a society can be a Joseph's coat of many diverse people, but they absolutely must have more in common than what separates them. We must share something with our neighbors besides a zip code.

> A diverse peaceful or stable society is against most historical precedent. ... It is much harder to achieve than most Americans acknowledge.

I am sobered by how much unity it takes. Look at the ancient Greeks. Philip Dorf's *Visualized World History* tells us: "The Greeks believed that they belonged to the same race; they possessed a common language and literature; and they worshiped the same gods. All Greece took part in the

Olympic games in honor of Zeus and all Greeks venerated the shrine of Apollo at Delphi. A common enemy, Persia, threatened their liberty. Yet, all of these bonds together were not strong enough to overcome two factors … [local patriotism and geographical conditions that nurtured political divisions]."

Our culture doesn't have to be (and shouldn't be) the culture of 1776 or 1950—but it must have a unified core. Tolerance and pluralism are not enough, in my mind, to keep a nation together. The history of multiple cultures living together without assimilation is not a happy history. Another scholar bluntly put it this way, "Americanization, then, although it did not cleanse America of its ethnic minorities, cleansed its minorities of their ethnicity." Blunt but true. We took Irish, Indians, and Italians, Cambodians and Chinese, Europeans and Ethiopians and made them into Americans. A nation must be more than a diverse people living in the same place and sharing only a standard of living. Today we take unprecedented numbers of immigrants, and we do so year after year. America faces a new and serious assimilation challenge.

I thus suggest that diversity is only an asset if it is secondary to unity. The emphasis must be on the *unum*, not the *pluribus*. We can be composed of many ethnic groups and religions, but we must be one nationality. We should respect diversity, but we should celebrate unity.

A Quality Community
Is One That Anticipates the Future.

A community must care about and anticipate its future. Citizens must anticipate major changes that will take place in their society. It must foresee and forestall. Public policy is like a kaleidoscope, and time turns it to present us with whole new patterns. America faces a new and potentially divisive issue in the aging of America, which threatens new tensions between young and old. It threatens to compound the tensions between various ethnic groups as a majority of minority workers pay 15.3 percent of their pay into Social Security and Medicare, the overwhelming recipients of which are elderly white Americans.

America is getting older—fast. In 1900, we could expect to live 47.3 years; by 2000, we could expect to reach the age of seventy-seven. It is likely those born early next century can expect to live to eighty-five. The over–sixty-five population for the last fifty years has been growing four times faster than the rest of the population. The United States today has more people over the age of sixty-five than Canada has people. In the next forty years, we will add more than 40 million people over sixty-five to the 31 million we presently have. This is essentially adding yet another Canada, plus all the people in the Rocky Mountain states to our elderly population.

Increased life expectancy is an asset to us individually, but not necessarily an asset to public policy. Compounding the increase in life expectancy and the sheer number of elderly, a third demographic revolution is taking place: the drop in the birthrate. People age from the moment they are born, but societies do not automatically age. Societies age mainly by a drop in the birthrate and an increase in longevity. This is what is happening in America and much of the world.

The results of this demographic change are in some ways predictable, in others unknowable. An emerging issue of great significance to Americans is intergenerational equity. We are not being fair to our children and our grandchildren; we are not paying debts that should rightly be ours; we are not leaving sustainable entitlement systems; and we are indulging ourselves at the expense of the future.

Laurence Kotlikoff and Scott Burns in their book *The Coming Generational Storm* point out that the fight for social justice between the haves and have-nots, while not solved, has evolved into a new issue, the have-nows versus the have-laters. We have to create justice not only within a generation, but also between different generations. We are failing on both counts, by neglecting to create social justice within our generation and now, additionally, by becoming the have-nows and pre-spending our children's money.

But the piper must eventually be paid. In the frightening tradition of Louis XV of France (whose mistress, Madame Pompadour, famously said, "*Après moi, le deluge*"), we have built a nation-threatening fiscal crisis into our children's future. In all cultures, in all nations, and in all religions, there is a universal theme against profligacy and for urging justice for future generations. A community cares about posterity. An old

Middle Eastern proverb observes, "The beginning of wisdom comes when a person plants a tree, the shade under which he knows he will never sit."

Wise words.

A Great Community Is One That Has Developed a Great Community Culture.

We need a community culture that gives diverse people a stake in each other. A community can celebrate differences, but its members must have a certain level of trust in each other and feel some sense of commitment toward each other. A community must have things they do or honor in common: voting, volunteering, donating blood, attending town meetings, trusting their neighbors and coworkers. There has to be a substantial degree of civic engagement in the community and some common loyalties.

America has come a long way since we questioned electing a Catholic president. It is not a stretch to imagine a woman, a black, or a Hispanic elected president this century. While increasingly we see minorities and women being elected in other countries, Harlan Cleveland challenges us to "try to imagine a Turkish Chancellor of Germany, an Algerian President of France, a Pakistani Prime Minister of Britain, a Christian President of Egypt, an Arab Prime Minister of Israel, a Jewish President of Syria, a Tibetan running China and anyone but a Japanese in power in Tokyo."

Amitai Etzioni says democracy occurs when we all fight with one arm tied behind our backs. A great community is one that has developed a great community culture.

A successful community culture encourages certain traits:

Citizen participation
Community leadership
Volunteerism and philanthropy
Civic education
Community pride
Justice

When Tocqueville visited America in the 1830s, he observed:

These Americans are a peculiar people. If, in a local community, a citizen becomes aware of a human need which is not being met, he thereupon discusses the situation with his neighbors. Suddenly a committee comes into existence. The committee thereupon begins to operate on behalf of the need and a new community function is established. It is like a miracle because these citizens perform this act without a single reference to any bureaucracy or any official agency.

He goes on to compare how Europe and America solved problems. He suggests that giving, volunteering, and joining are mutually reinforcing and habit forming, what Tocqueville called "habits of the heart." In Europe, he said, they would wait for the king or prince or government to fix it. In America, he observed, people would form an association and solve the problem themselves.

A community must have adequate social capital. Physical capital is our physical infrastructure: roads, bridges, and water systems; social capital is the social networks: the habits of neighborliness and patriotism, the trust we develop with working and relating to others. It is the whole network of reciprocal social relations.

A Community Needs a Strong Collective Identity, Including a Shared Culture and Shared Language.

John Gardner says, "If the community is lucky, and fewer and fewer are, it will have a shared history and tradition ... which it will use to heighten its members' sense of belonging." He goes on to say, "To maintain the sense of belonging and the dedication and commitment so essential to community life, members need inspiring reminders of shared goals and values."

> I am convinced that one of the shared values we must have is a shared language.

I am convinced that one of the shared values we must have is a shared language. It is a blessing for an individual to be bilingual; it is a curse for a society to be bilingual. We need a common currency so we can pay our debts to each other in understandable form, and we must likewise be able to articulate our differences and celebrate our commonalties with a shared language. Members of a society must be able to talk to each other and avoid competing languages, which have so haunted

Quebec. One scholar, Seymour Martin Lipset, put it this way, "The histories of bilingual and bicultural societies that do not assimilate are histories of turmoil, tension, and tragedy. Canada, Belgium, Malaysia, Lebanon—all face crises of national existence in which minorities press for autonomy, if not independence. Pakistan and Cyprus have divided. Nigeria suppressed an ethnic rebellion. France faces difficulties with its Basques, Bretons, and Corsicans."

The United States is at a crossroads. One out of five U.S. residents—nearly 47 million people—speak a language other than English at home, according to the U.S. Census Bureau. An estimated 28 million people use Spanish as their primary language. We must move toward either greater integration or toward more fragmentation. We will either have to assimilate much better all of the peoples within our boundaries, or we will see an increasing alienation and fragmentation. Bilingual and bicultural nations are inherently unstable. We found in the 1950s that separate was inherently unequal. We must find that separate is also inherently divisive.

Thou Shall Not Ask What Your Community Can Do for You. Thou Shall Ask What You Can Do for Your Community.

A quality community is one that balances rights and privileges with duties and responsibilities. No society can live on rights and privileges alone, and we have tried too long. Our community and our nation—which nurtured us—now need something in return. A community must demand some duties and responsibilities from its citizens. We must ask, What we can do for our community?

Just as a boat needs a sail and an anchor, a community needs freedom and some restriction on that freedom. Freedom is a wonderful idea, but it does not trump all other considerations. Saul Bellow postulates that "America is as threatened by an excess of liberty as Russia was by the absence of liberty." Those are important words. I quoted earlier the wise words of an eighteenth-century philosopher who observed that "Freedom is the luxury of self-discipline." Passing laws will not keep a nation great if it does not have a culture of honesty, justice, compassion, hard work, and discipline.

> Just as a boat needs a sail and an anchor, a community needs freedom and some restriction on that freedom.

"America, the Beautiful" mirrors that same thought when it says, "Confirm thy soul in self-control thy liberty in law." A free republic demands a far higher degree of virtue than any earlier society. It demands a profound sense of personal responsibility, a willingness to govern one's own passions, a capacity for initiative and self-reliance, a taste for personal independence, and a sustained spirit of civic cooperation.

> We cannot ever pass enough laws and ordinances to substitute for a sense of civic virtue.

In short, tolerance in moderation becomes a safety net. Tolerance stretched too far becomes loosely woven fabric where the holes are larger than the strings are strong—a net that invites the criminals and the narrow moralists rather than the truly moral to rush in. We cannot ever pass enough laws and ordinances to substitute for a sense of civic virtue. Communities need standards as well as laws.

An old Presbyterian hymn out of my youth reflects my concern about the present status of community:

New occasions teach new duties.
Time makes ancient good uncouth.

Community is both an ancient and modern good. But we can no longer take community for granted in the United States. We have too much evidence that we are unraveling and becoming unglued. There is too much tension, too much misunderstanding, too many separate tribes yelling at each other. Our civic dialogue is too often a dialogue between the blind and the deaf. It is dangerous, and we must attempt to salvage that elusive concept of community. We can create chaos, as in Bosnia, or we can create community. It is up to us.

Chapter Six
What Does It Mean to Our Future?

We Must Expand the Dialogue.

America's future and unity as a nation are at risk because of our reluctance to talk honestly and candidly about race and ethnicity. We have been intimidated too long by the very real fear of being charged with racism.

Equally important, we are doing the black and Hispanic community a great disservice by our silence. Every group has the ability to take its place fully in American history. It is not lack of talent or some inherent inferiority that too often results in underperformance or failure, it is lack of values in a supportive cultural context. Culture has the power to overcome discrimination, poverty, even racism if it sends the right signals. Yet I have come to believe that in America, minorities will have to own more of their own problems if they are to succeed. American success is open to

> It is not lack of talent or some inherent inferiority that too often results in underperformance or failure, it is lack of values in a supportive cultural context.

all as never before in American society. Blacks and Hispanics have to transition from seeking the solution to their underperformance in the broader society to an inner journey of self-exploration and self-improvement. These observations are from someone who cares.

I was elected governor of Colorado in 1974 and took my seat in 1975. My lieutenant governor, George Brown, was Colorado's first black official elected on a statewide basis and one of the first black lieutenant governors in the nation. Both of us had a passionate interest in the education of minority kids and particularly the troubling drop-out rate in both the black and Hispanic communities. We would meet regularly, one or both, with the black and Hispanic members of the legislature and discuss this problem and the solutions.

Our administration started a number of initiatives in education, but those dealing with black and Hispanic students were particularly frustrating. For our Hispanic students, we initiated English as a Second Language (ESL) programs. Little or no improvement followed. I next asked the legislature for, and signed, the first bilingual education legislation in Colorado. I was persuaded that this was the route to success for our Hispanic children. It was repealed a few years later by our Republican legislature, but on what seemed good grounds: there was no evidence that it was working. By the time I signed its repeal, I had come to see bilingual education as more a political agenda than an educational reform.

The minority legislators claimed that Anglo teachers were "tracking" Hispanic students, so we helped the Denver School District create an all-Hispanic school with a Hispanic principal and Hispanic teachers. Same sad story. Same sad drop-out rate.

I grew increasingly frustrated, not only because we couldn't find the key to success, but also increasingly because the only area the black and Hispanic caucuses would talk about was racism and discrimination. Any failure on the part of minority community must, per se, be the fault of the larger society. As a former civil rights attorney, that message resonated at first, but soon became an inadequate explanation for the total problem we were facing. Yes, there was racism and discrimination left in our society, but was that the sole cause for the educational failure that so plagued these two communities? I have been bothered by this lack of candid dialogue for thirty years.

Belatedly, that dialogue is starting. There is a common theme emerging among a few minority leaders and a much more developed dialogue from South American and African intellectuals that nations and groups have to stop making so many excuses and must look to self reliance and self-improvement for their salvation. This dialogue doesn't preclude the continuing effort to examine other contributing factors, but the major thrust must turn from "the enemy without" to "the enemy within."

America's top Hispanic business leader, Lionel Sosa, says the Hispanic community is being held back by "cultural shackles." And, similarly, Thomas Sowell warns that blacks are "crippled by their culture." He asks:

Why are so many of black alumni of Harvard either from the West Indies or Africa, or children of these two groups? If America is a racist society, why do we give a pass to Blacks from these areas? We don't, they come from cultures that haven't been crippled by the excuse of victimization. Slavery was the sad experience of both blacks in America and the West Indies, but the culture of the West Indies would not allow its children to make excuses for themselves.

Listen to black Professor Shelby Steele, who says of the black community, "Our great problem today is insufficient development more than white racism" and warns that blacks "will have no real power without taking responsibility for their own educational and economic development." "It is now our turn to step up the plate," he tells fellow blacks. "Opportunity follows struggle. It follows effort. It follows hard work. It doesn't come before. The Promised Land guarantees nothing. It is only an opportunity, not a deliverance. ... It is time for blacks to begin the shift from a wartime to a peacetime identity, from fighting for opportunity to the seizing of it."

Steele says, "It is damned near impossible for a Black person to act as an individual anymore, so oppressed are we by the expectations of our group identity as protesting victims."

White institutions throughout our society are terrified of the charge of so-called racism, as I experienced at the University of Denver. It haunts much of what goes on throughout the campuses. It infects course selection and the selection of material within many courses. Don't discuss anything that might be interpreted as critical of minorities, for you will be hit broadside with charges of racism. Unfortunately, the result of this taboo is clearly to harm minorities, not help them. The white community is excusing poor performance and acting like they have to prove they are not racist by disallowing anything that is even mildly critical of black and Hispanic America, no matter how well motivated or well founded. White America is only supposed to blame itself.

Consequently, issues of great importance to America's future are being muted, downplayed, or censored because people dread being politically incorrect or, even worse, being called racist. White America is partially paralyzed in discussing some of the most important issues to America's future.

Our Silence Is Harming the Minority Community.

Even more important, the effect is to deny black and Hispanic America the wisdom that other groups have obtained about advancing in our society. Too many in the black and Hispanic leadership think salvation lies in group identity and pushing for group rights, not in individual merit. Shelby Steele, for instance, warns that when group identity, not individual merit, becomes the raison d'être of the black agenda, the resulting concentration on victimization prevents the minority community from looking inward, and relief comes solely from the guilt of the white community, not from self-advancement and self-help.

Black America is suffering from an epidemic of out-of-wedlock births. We know enough about family dynamics to know the damage done to children raised without a father or other male role models in the home. Yes, some children seem to survive it, but these are

> Too many in the black and Hispanic leadership think salvation lies in group identity and pushing for group rights, not in individual merit.

the exceptions that prove the rule. Every social pathology in a society, whether high crime rates, high school drop-out rates, a high occurrence of teenage pregnancy, or low performance in school, is more present in single-mother and single-father households. It is hard to write a happy scenario for the black community if over two-thirds of its births continue to be out-of-wedlock births. To not speak candidly is to cheat these children and perpetuate the problem.

In his 1958 book, *Stride Toward Freedom*, Martin Luther King Jr. made an immensely important point, "In short, we must work on two fronts. On the one hand, we must continue to resist the system which is the basic cause of our lagging standards; on the other hand, we must work constructively to improve the standards themselves. There must be a rhythmic alternation between attacking the causes and healing the effects."

Wise words, even more applicable today.

Appendix A
Typology of Progress-Prone
and Progress-Resistant Cultures

A fusion of the ideas of Mariano Grondona, Lawrence
Harrison, Matteo Marini, and Irakli Chkonia

	Factor	Progress-Prone Culture	Progress-Resistant Culture
WORLDVIEW	1. Religion	Nurtures rationality, achievement; promotes material pursuits; focus on this world; pragmatism	Nurtures irrationality; inhibits material pursuits; focus on the other world; utopianism
	2. Destiny	I can influence my destiny for the better	Fatalism, resignation, sorcery
	3. Time orientation	Future focus promotes planning, punctuality, deferred gratification	Present or past focus discourages planning, punctuality, saving
	4. Wealth	Product of human creativity	What exists (zero-sum)
	5. Knowledge	Practical, verifiable; facts matter	Abstract, theoretical, cosmological, not verifiable; debate matters

Factor	Progress-Prone Culture	Progress-Resistant Culture
VALUES, VIRTUES		
6. Ethical code	Rigorous within realistic norms; feeds trust	Elastic, wide gap between utopian norms and behavior = mistrust
7. The lesser virtues	A job well done, tidiness, courtesy, punctuality matter	Lesser virtues unimportant; love, justice, courage matter
8. Education	Indispensable; promotes autonomy	Less priority; promotes dependency, orthodoxy
ECONOMIC BEHAVIOR		
9. Work/achievement	Live to work; work leads to wealth	Work to live; work doesn't lead to wealth; work is for the poor
10. Frugality	The mother of investment and prosperity	A threat to equality
11. Entrepreneurship	Investment and creativity	A threat to equality
12. Risk propensity	Moderate	Low; occasional adventures
13. Competition	Leads to excellence	Aggression; a threat to equality and privilege
14. Innovation	Open; rapid adaptation	Suspicious; slow adaptation
15. Advancement	Merit, achievement	Family, patron, connections
16. Rule of law/corruption	Reasonably law abiding; corruption is prosecuted	Money, connections matter; corruption is tolerated
17. Radius of identification and trust	Stronger identification with the broader society	Stronger identification with the narrow community
18. Association (social capital)	Trust, identification breed cooperation, affiliation, participation	Mistrust breeds excessive individualism, anomie
19. The individual/the group	Emphasizes the individual, but not excessively	Emphasizes the collectivity
20. Authority	Dispersed; checks and balances, consensus	Centralized; unfettered, often arbitrary
21. Role of elites	Responsibility to society	Power and rent seeking; exploitative
22. Church-state relations	Secularized; wall between church and state	Religion plays major role in civic sphere

Appendix B
Books That Speak Volumes

The subject of culture, however controversial, has recently found myriad supporters. *Culture Matters: How Values Shape Human Progress*, edited by Lawrence Harrison and Samuel Huntington (Basic Books, 2000), is a collection of twenty-two essays written by a number of scholars and commentators who are looking to culture as a prime determinant in the success of various people. These essays generally urge the reader to look at culture as *the* significant factor in the economic, educational, and political success of various peoples. David Landes in his essay repeats the findings of his influential book *The Wealth and Poverty of Nations* (W. W. Norton & Company, 1997), in which he states that "Culture makes all the difference in the economic success of peoples and nations."

Harrison's earlier book, *Underdevelopment Is a State of Mind* (Madison Books, 1985), compares different countries and how their culture helps explain the difference in their respective advancement and development. So many of the problems of South and Central America can be found in the culture of those who conquered it 500 years ago. This is one of the most influential books I have ever read. A reinforcing Hispanic viewpoint can be found in *The Americano Dream: How Latinos Can Achieve Success in Business and in Life* by Lionel Sosa (Plume, 1998). Sosa's purpose in writing this book was to share his almost forty years of business experience with other Latinos. He feels the subject of culture is so important that he titled his first chapter "Escaping the Cultural Shackles." Similarly, we must "look beyond the classroom" to subjects such as culture, states Laurence Steinberg in his book *Beyond the Classroom: Why School Reform Has Failed and What Parents Need to Do* (Touchstone, 1996).

A complementary viewpoint for the black community is put forth in *Losing the Race: Self-Sabotage in Black America* by John H. McWhorter (The Free Press, 2000). McWhorter identifies three manifestations for "the ideological sea of troubles plaguing black America, all self inflicted": The Cult of Victimology (to treat victimhood not as a problem to be solved, but as an identity to be nurtured), Separatism ("a natural outgrowth of victimology"), and Anti-Intellectualism (where to do well is considered "acting white" by much of the black community). McWhorter states that "These three currents hold black Americans back from the true freedom that so many consider whites to be denying them."

In *Trust: The Social Virtues and the Creation of Prosperity* by Francis Fukuyama (The Free Press, 1995), the author asks, "What is the most important factor in the economic success of a new baby born today anywhere in the world? Is it how it is raised? How it is educated? Who its parents are? What are its genes?" None of the above, says Fukuyama: The most important correlation to that baby's economic success is "What culture the baby is born into." A powerful, provocative book.